CW00617786

Contemplations
of the Heart

Contemplations
of the Heart

A BOOK OF MALE SPIRIT

PHOTOGRAPHY, DIGITAL IMAGING AND TEXT

by

Peter Grahame

Peter Grahame

Published by

Ironic Horse Studio
Ironic Horse, Inc.
Albuquerque, NM
Printed in Korea by Palace Press International
www.palacepress.com

Published by Peter Grahame, Ironic Horse Studio, Ironic Horse, Inc.
416 Iron Ave. SE, Albuquerque, NM 87102-3937, (505) 924-2161
www.ironic-horse.com

First edition limited to 2000 hard bound copies, 2005
ISBN #0-9774278-0-3 and #978-0-9774278-0-2
Library of Congress Control Number: 2005909567

Contents

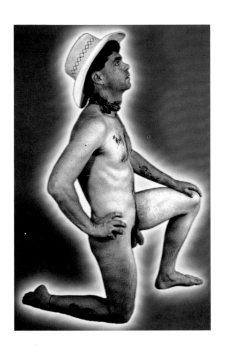

Dedication

This book is dedicated to my life partner, Henry Seale.
Thank you, Henry, for your patience, your constant
encouragement, and your unending unconditional Love
these twenty years. You are truly a Magnificent Spirit,
the center of my heart.

I also dedicate this book to all the men who lead
in the Male Spirit Movements, Gay and Straight
and everyone in between,
because you do so much
to help heal the wounds
and to create a new way of being.

And to all our bold and truly courageous
Male Spirit Ancestors.
We are this far because of them.

And finally, this book is dedicated to you,
searcher, dreamer, lover of life.

Acknowledgments

I would like to thank all of the exceptional guys who presented their Inner Spirit to my camera. We made these images together.

Thanks to:
- Troy • John • Joe • Dean • Jon-Carl • Keith •
- Raven • Bill • Hunter • David • Dimid •
- Rob & Chris • Gary • Gabe • Taka • Charles •
- Michael • Ron • Steven • 3Raven • Ragiligir •
- William • Rand • Hans & Ian • Julian • Kenny •
- VanGuard • Marqis • Randy • Bob • Jim • Henry •
- Estevan • Colt • Rev • Stephen • David J. •
- and Anonymous •

• All the persons appearing in this book are over 18 years of age. Photo releases on file with the artist. Appearance in this book does not necessarily imply a person's sexual orientation.

• Please note: Although I do only present male images here, and I do only use the words Gay or Straight, my intention is to refer to any male however he wishes to describe himself, including Bisexual, Faery, Queer, Questioning, Two-Spirit, or Transgender. There is no intention to leave anyone out. I apologize for any mistakes in references.

• I apologize for there not being any men represented in this book who are "disabled" or "differently abled." To include that aspect of Spirit in this book was my intention; I made an effort, but the connection did not take place. Perhaps it will for the next book. Yet I trust that perhaps those who do identify with those terms can find meaning for themselves in here, as well.

Introduction

This book started out as a couple of hand bound volumes with prints glued in and text printed on my computer. Good friends called it a labor of love and I suppose it is. The book was also passed around to men on Gay retreats, Straight retreats, and even to men at a Native people's ceremony were it was acknowledged and blessed by a two-spirit elder.

It generally received favorable comments in that form. The one thing men, Gay or Straight, say they appreciate most about the book is that it presents ordinary guys as they are—various ages, shapes, sizes, colors—just guys. Sensual, maybe a little erotic, but not overly idealized or objectified sexually, and without the emphasis on "youth cult"—and in a transcendental or transformational context. Metaphors of the Spirit. Certainly non-aggressive. A more "subject-to-subject" approach, as Gay freedom

forerunner Harry Hay might have said. Ordinary guys in extraordinary settings. Dream images. The workings of my "intuitive consciousness" perhaps. It's difficult to describe. But most of the men who viewed the book said they discovered a reflection of themselves in it, and here and there found meaning in the text

The ideas expressed with these images, of course, are just my thoughts and opinions. Perhaps it's me speaking, or the image speaking, or maybe it's Spirit speaking. Or maybe it's your own subconscious speaking. Naturally, you may read the text any way you like, or just ignore it. Besides, they're really not "my thoughts," anyway. I read and study and glean ideas from

Buddhism, mystical Christianity, metaphysical thought and other spiritual philosophies, but I'm hardly an expert; just a curious searcher, looking for meaning, and these ideas have more or less come together here. I don't pretend to live up to everything I've written. They're just ideas I believe to be true. Living it takes constant practice.

Anyway, to the images. What are they? Why did I make them with these guys? Well, my idea is to express something about us that may not have been fully expressed before. Something about positive self-image and doing away with self-hatred and internalized homophobia. I want to help heal the Gay Male Spirit and to indicate to any man, Gay or Straight, his sacred inner self, his integral connection to the on-going process of creation, and his responsibility to cherish the earth and all who are on it. This is also about refusing to objectify each other, sexually or otherwise, and developing honest and open subject-to-subject relationships. It's also an attempt to change the notion that only certain images of idealized youth or physical appearance are acceptable. We're all acceptable. What's more, I'd like to further the idea that Gay men, especially, by their nature, do have a distinctive view of the world, of spirituality, and that we have certain abilities for healing, for ritual, and for transformation that can and should be offered to the larger culture from which we spring. My hope is that this book presents a group of meditations on these sincere ideals.

When I do another book, it will be about Queer Spirit Archetypes, and it will be in collaboration with a woman and a transgendered person. This book is about males, and most certainly with an emphasis on our multi-gendered aspects, opening up to the Sacred Feminine in us, which can only lead to a deeper respect for women. I personally think ideas like these are very important for us to consider if we're to continue to truly evolve...

In the end, what I want to say is that I have the greatest, deepest respect for all of the guys who were willing to be naked in front of my camera. I am truly grateful that they were so willing to openly present their inner selves; and because they were so open, they really did help create these images. What's more, I believe these images are concerned not with self-absorption but with self-reflection. I know the images reflect me, and the guys reflect themselves. We can only bring about change in the world by starting with ourselves. Only when we self-reflect can we change within, find inner peace, and then connect with others, turning to a genuine sense of active compassion.

In any case, these men and I also had a lot of fun making these images. I hope you'll enjoy them for what they are, and maybe find something in them for yourself, and for your own contemplations of your own heart. In Buddhist traditions, the word *bodhicitta* means "awakened heart." Through honest self-contemplation, one awakens the heart to the self. Self knowledge leads to active identification with and compassion for others, which leads to appreciation of the true gift, the true joy, of being alive.

My most heartfelt intention is that these images help each of us wake up just a little more, because all of us waking up is exactly what it's going to take for our fragile world in turmoil to come to a new time of peace —a new time when it is finally understood that Love is, in fact, the answer to everything.

~ Peter Grahame, Albuquerque, NM, October, 2005

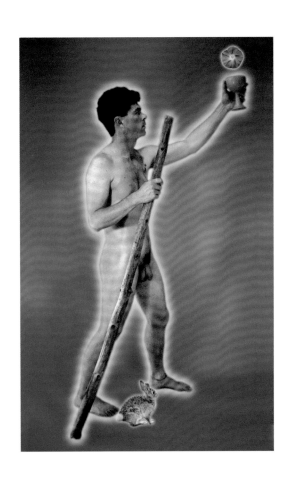

Flower
and
Flame

The Rose of the Soul opens
when the Inner Light is right.

My Soul is the Gentle Sentry of my Being.
Not to guard, but to witness: That there is
nothing and everything to lose;
everything and nothing to gain.

Flowing with life is moving in peace with life,
as it is.

What am I protecting?
There are no boundaries.
When the flower opens the bee attends.

Within every body is a sacred heart.

Having the serenity of a saint simply means
that I mindfully, peacefully
do whatever there is to do
in the moment.

Am I climbing
a ladder of
detachment?
Or indifference?
If I'm fortunate
enough to ascend
and learn,
then I can return
and use what I learn
for others.

9

Politically, to be silent
is to die. Spiritually, to be
silent is to find my inner fire.

But that's where all
political change originates.

Within.

When I accept who I am as I am, as easily as the lily accepts the bee, Love manifests. Transformation takes place. For myself, others, the earth.

How could sin possibly have
anything to do with making Love?

Honestly, making *Love*...

Sin is deliberately hurting
another human being
through conscious action or inaction.
None of that happens here.

So no matter what others in the world may say,
we know we are Love.

Anger is fear, uncontrolled force, self-indulgent;
anger destroys, debilitates, leads to remorse...
If I will understand anger, I can eliminate it.
What is left? Assertive compassion.

Although the Truth of Love is incomprehensible,
Love is found in every solitary heart.

It is the essence of my being. It is my rock. My fire.
It is what I have to give.

There are billions, *billions* of us
on this planet. The numbers may be
staggering, the suffering overwhelming,
but here is another astounding thought:
Each of us is a gesture of Love.
That means that no matter who I am
or where I am, no matter what
the condition of my life, I can say,
"Here is where Love begins, here in me."

Natural
Transformations

When I find the magic
of my inner peace,
I cannot stay isolated
in the upper room of my mind.

Forget the past. What am I doing
with the rest of my life?
Divine Mother Father, give me the courage
to step through the further door.

Emerging from a cage I built myself...

I know I am alive in all worlds at once. No birth, no death,
just life, everywhere. Healing is in the way I live my life. So if
I die today, I know I have lived, will still live, somewhere,
always watching, being aware.

There is meaning in the morning light.
There is awareness in every step.

With the old abused ideas of sacrifice and suffering, real grace is lost.

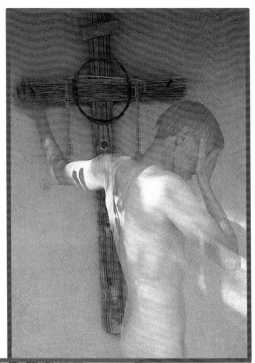

Divine Love says there is an amazing grace found in nature.
A constant resurrection, an ever new spirit.

Yes, we *can* heal ourselves. And real healing can take place if we will fully and completely open our hearts to each other. Imagine what the earth would be like...

Within every man is a Pan,
a Green Man, deeply, joyfully,
connected to the earth.

If I can't see the beauty in growing older, then I'll keep struggling to stay young, a fearful and pointless task. After all, each step is the first step on the journey that never ends. Love making never ends either.

I can only give my elder wisdom effectively
if I realize that the young have much to teach me.

Not causing harm requires staying awake
in the present moment.

Watching. Aware. Mindful. Ready.

Being fearless means being able to go *beyond* fear.
Breathe, know that Love is stronger, and take a step.

Contemplations
of the Heart

Only when I can enter into
the clear contemplation of my own Heart
can I begin to understand
my connection to all things.

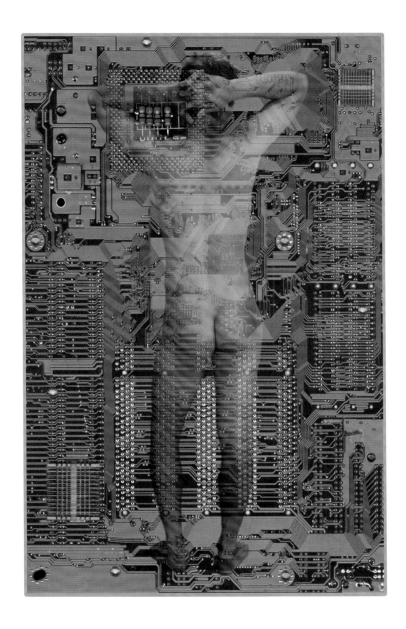

In our world manipulated by the computer and the Internet
how do I connect with my self? I hear my soul calling in this
wilderness. Yet how much do I participate in the chaos?
Change begins when I change my patterns.

The overwhelming insight is that I am *me* and I am *you*!
I *am* connected to all things! This incomprehensible
sense of oneness is a terrifying idea!
And a truly liberating thought.

A very great teacher
said, essentially:

If I can understand
and pay attention
to being alive,
alive in every way,
   without judgement,
   without greed, without
   anger and ambition;
   without sorrow, despair,
   fear, and a sense of loss...

      only then can I know
      Love as my true source;
      only then can I light
         the way for myself;
      and only then can I be
   of true service to others.

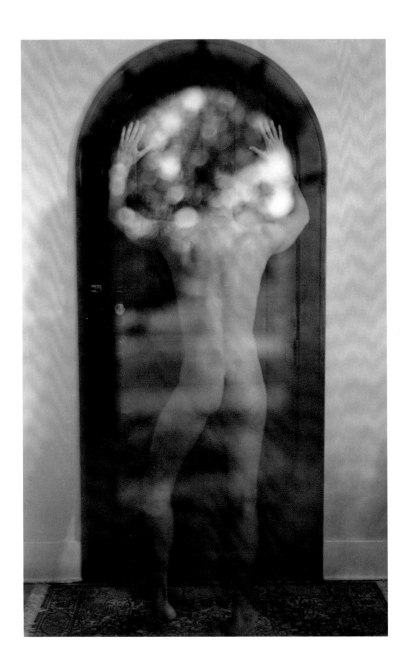

To get through
the doorway
to my dreams
I just have to

open it.

What is it like to be
spontaneously compassionate?
To not be weighed down by
the burden of choice, of condescension,
of some mandate of social consciousness,
but to actually act immediately out of Love?

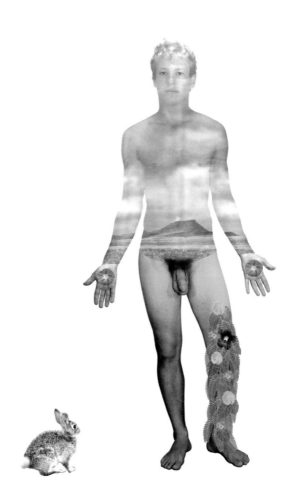

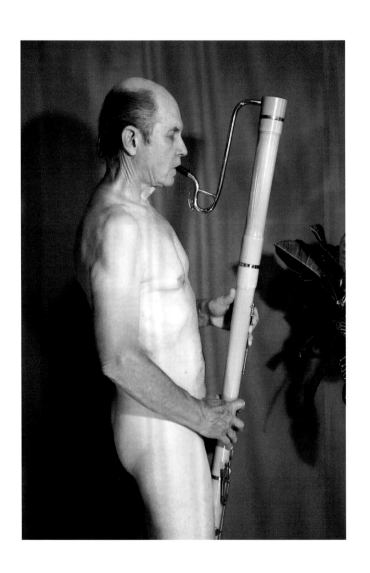

Love
surrounds me
in my waking moments,
and in the hours I dream.
Love is why I am.

Who am I?
How did I come to be?
Why am I here?
These are questions
the animals never seem to ask.
Yet they live
in certain balance.
That is what I learn from them.
That is why I have respect
and compassion
for all living things.

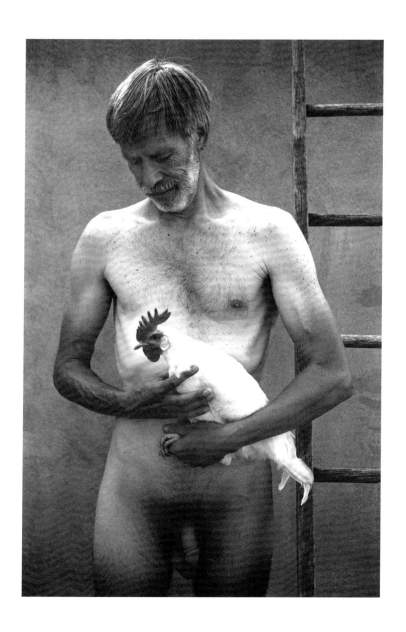

Awakenings

The first thing to do
when I'm called
to awaken is to...

wake up.

Only when I awaken
and accept myself
can I begin to think
of helping another
to awaken, too.

Together we create
one new
vessel,
a new
Self,
willing
to be
filled
with Life.

The world is in such sad turmoil. Are all the gods asleep? I can't wait for the gods to wake up. I have to wake up to myself and get busy. I know I can't save the whole world, but I can start right where I am. An end to turmoil in myself creates peace right where I am. And that peace really does change the whole world.

In fact, compared to millions in the world, I am privileged. I have a *responsibility* to wake up. To work in my garden; plant and water it. Nurture my spirit. Grow my own soul. To make the decision to be free from anxiety; to be joyful, grateful, useful, and willing to do the work. The rewards blossom constantly. And the more they bloom, the more I can give away.

How much longer can we continue to do what we do to the Earth? Yet the Earth can indeed go on without us; it is we who are the guests here. Whoever I am, wherever I am, in any way that I can, I can start now to cherish the Earth as a gift, and help the Earth come to a new beginning.

The Vehicle can be
a symbol for the Body.
Mind and Spirit need to pull
in the same direction.
But I'm in the driver's seat,
the Star of my own road movie.
Where am I going?
What am I doing
with my living energy?
Don't fall asleep at the wheel.
Don't look back.
The adventure is in every
moment of the way.

And a benefit to being
really awake and alive is
no fear of death.

Why not create my own
cultural symbols for

Gender.
Race.
Sex.
Religion.
Age.
Country.

All of it. Fluid.

Maybe what we're
really afraid of is
not death, but
radical rebirth.

A completely new
way of seeing.
A totally new way
of being.

What would total freedom be like?
No restrictive concepts.
No definitive beliefs.
No stigmas.
No repressions.
Only the very essence of equality.
In flaming color.

If we can imagine, indeed,
what it would be like...
we can make it happen.

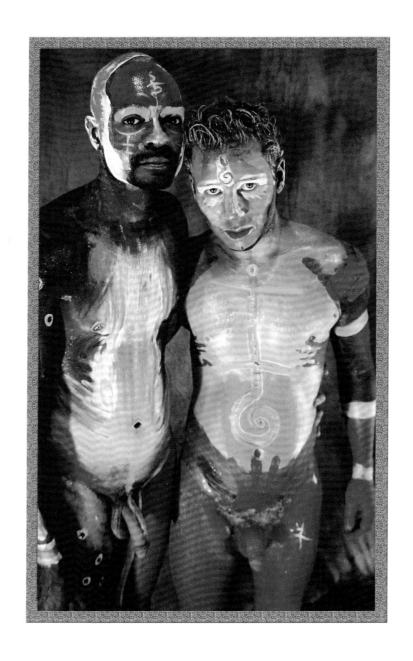

Instead of a Dark Night of the Soul,
let us experience a Bright Night of the Spirit!
If we keep a star handy, the night will reveal much...
For out of the void all is created.

And the dawn brings a new light. So, instead of Spirit Warriors,
let us be Spirit Dancers. Letting go! Rejoicing!
For the sun is rising, and the bee is dancing on the lily...
Magic is in every moment we live.

After Words

About the process: This book represents nearly 10 years of creating photographs, and later, digital images, with some 75 men. 40 of them are presented here, several two or three times. All of the images in this book were created with a 35 mm Canon® camera, using various films. They were lit with either natural light outside, or using ordinary spotlights and other light sources in the studio space. Negatives, slides and sometimes prints were scanned on an Epson® 1600 and brought into Adobe® Photoshop®. I created all the digital images this way using my own photography, montaging photos and so on, almost never using any stock images. Sometimes I scanned in frame edges, hand drawn art work, or real objects. The font is Adobe® PostScript™ Baker Signet.

~

Virtually all of the images can be produced as high quality digital prints using fine archival paper and inks. These prints are available in several sizes.

If you'd like information about pricing and how you can obtain prints of these images, please contact me through the information given below.

Peter Grahame
Ironic Horse Studio
416 Iron Ave. SE
Albuquerque, NM 87102-3937

(505) 924-2161

www.ironic-horse.com

Here is a list of all of the images by page, title and, in most cases, the name of the subject of the image. All images © 2005, Peter Grahame, Ironic Horse Studio, Ironic Horse, Inc.

About the Artist

Self taught, Peter Grahame began his art making in 1982 by creating masks for the theater and as wall sculptures. He also created mixed media works using his own photography with found objects, and he experimented with fabric art. Later, he found he really enjoyed making these transformational

photographs with his naked friends, and this led to his more recent digital imaging. "Whatever I create, it's about spiritual discovery," he says. He makes photos of nature and the technological world, as well. His work has been presented in numerous theatrical productions, and in many gallery exhibits in the Chicago area and in New Mexico. Peter has worked as an actor, director, advertising writer, designer and art teacher. He lives with his life partner, Henry Seale, in Albuquerque. They own and operate Ironic Horse Studio in their home. Henry plays and teaches the Renaissance recorder, so their gallery studio home is always filled with music, art... peace.

Oh, yes, the bunny. A cross-cultural icon, he is clever, prolific, creative, yet so vulnerable, too; the symbol for Everyman, a witness to this inner work.

"Is that him?" "I think that's him." "Yeah, that's him."

83

It's difficult to
accept that the
life I lead
may be over at
any moment.
But when I do realize it,
a deep appreciation
for life, just as it is,
each moment, in all I do,
washes over me
and I can
experience joy
ever present,
and pass it on
to others.